In All Things, Love
Escaping the Church Schism Cycle

By Jimmie D. Compton, Jr.,

Dedication

To my great-grandsons, Ahmad and
Ahmir Thorns, "I love you!". You always bring
joy to my soul!

Publisher's Cataloging-in-Publication Data

Compton, Jimmie Davis, Jr., 1951-

In All Things, Love, Escaping the Church Schism Cycle / Jimmie Davis Compton, Jr.

ISBN: 978-0-940123-08-3

This is a reflection of current events within the Christian church in America among Christian nationalist, Christian activist and carnal Christians. Infamous similarities to church schisms during the 4th through 5th century A.D. are cited, as well as cautions about the possibility of similar outcomes. A well-known perspective to be embraced by American Christians that potentially could lead to a Church unified under the primacy of Jesus' kingdom message is offered.

First Edition

Cover photo: By Jimmie D. Compton, Jr.

Table of Contents

Introduction

Natalie Wolchover's August 5, 2011 article on livescience.com entitled *Why Do Humans Walk in Circles?* It states

> When lost in the desert or a thick forest terrain devoid of landmarks people tend to walk in circles. Blindfolded people show the same tendency; lacking external reference points, they curve around in loops as tight as 66 feet (20 meters) in diameter, all the while believing they are walking in straight lines.
>
> Why can't we walk straight?
>
> Only recently have scientists begun to make gains in answering this age-old question. By conducting a series of experiments with blindfolded test subjects, a group of researchers at the Max Planck Institute for Biological Cybergenetics in Germany have systematically ruled out several plausible explanations for loopy walking. For example, body asymmetries has been posed as one theory, but the team found no correlation between factors such as uneven leg lengths and right- or left-side dominance and walkers' veering directions.

Similarly, to keep believers from a circular walk of faith, the Bible offers spiritual landmarks that lead us to progressively mature in faith. Jesus says in John 14:6, "... I am the way and the truth and the life..." Heeding His teachings not only leads to a purposeful life, but it also keeps us from repeating mistakes we made in the past.

Below is the beginning of several triggers of mental notes. The hope is that these statements and questions will help you remain intentional about heeding the teachings of Jesus. As you reflect on your replies, you can also use the space provided to write brief notes.

MENTAL NOTE #1: Which believer(s) in the Bible repeated past mistakes.

MENTAL NOTE #2: Reflect on past mistakes that you tend to repeat.

Chapter 1: Ears That Hear

Intentional listening, to the wise counsel of spiritually mature believers, can also provide some "just in time" landmarks to follow ... as the book Titus chapter 2 urges. If we are going to understand what we hear the mature say, then in addition to being intentional, it is particularly important to be attentive. We don't want to simply hear on a subliminal level.

But being intentional has its pitfalls, such as differences in vocabulary levels (between the speaker and hearer), and contextual assumptions (the ability to derive meaning for context). Every person has at least three vocabularies: one for interpreting what he is hearing or reading, another for used when speaking, and one used when writing. Intentional listening requires the use of our interpretive vocabulary. That is, words we understand by themselves, as well as the words we understand based upon other words used in the context. I need not explain how vital it is to understand what we hear. In Mark 8:17-18, Jesus lets us in on another consideration that affects how we interpret what we hear. Depending on the predisposition of the heart, grave misunderstandings can result.

So, it behooves both the speaker and hearer to recognize these pitfalls as possible obstacles to understanding. This is of particular importance in today's highly contested views on constitutional application, biblical interpretations, social justice and equality. Why? Because the opposing parties often use the same terminology to express their viewpoints. When, in fact, something radically different may lie in the context, or in the intent of the speaker's heart, or in the way the hearer interprets the message.

Therefore, the hearts and ears of 21st century Christians must first be honed to our oneness, as the body of Christ, apart from the various voices from our politics, fears, pleasures and pride. Today's religious-political disunity is a repeat of the church split during the 4th through 5th centuries A.D.; that was followed by the demise of Christianity in North Africa. Prior to the split, not even the certainty of death could keep the Apostles, Polycarp, Ignatius, Leonides, Namphanio, Cyprian, and many others from remaining a unified whole as the church – throughout what is now Africa, Europe, and the Middle-East.

MENTAL NOTE #3: What reason did Jesus give for His disciples' failure to understanding the miracle of the loaves and fish?

MENTAL NOTE #4: How might the reason above cause them to repeat mistakes in the future?

Chapter 2: Listen to Understand

By implication, Jesus suggests that our heart influences how we interpret what's heard. Therefore, when what's heard is related to the kingdom of God, it is critical that we evaluate our hearts before acting on our interpretation. That is no small task! It's difficult to do because our hearts want what they want, simply because we have invested so much in putting what's there. Besides, reacting to what is heard often occurs within a nanosecond. There is not enough time to insert an intermediate step to evaluate our heart. Usually, we have already reacted upon hearing what we have heard.

Been there, done that.

But on second thought, inserting such an intermediate step is something we already know how to do. Take our time in grade school for example, we intentionally inserted such a step. Then eventually, it became tacit – *know-how* gained through experience that is often difficult to explain. Consider the following two-word categories, and a few terms, to show how we moved from intentionality to tacit knowledge.

First, consider the category of words called homophonic homonyms. These are words that have the same pronunciation but different meanings and are spelled differently. For example, the words *they're (t-h-e-y-'-r-e)*, *their (t-h-e-i-r)*, and *there (t-h-e-r-e)*, or the word *break (b-r-e-a-k)* and *brake (b-r-a-k-e)*. Upon hearing them in grade school, we intentionally inserted a step to discern their particular meaning from the sentence's context.

Next, the category of words called homographic homonyms. These are words that share the same spelling but have more than one meaning and sometimes can have different pronunciations. For example, the words *season, bank,* or *lead.* As with homophonic homonyms, we discerned their meaning from the sentence's context.

What I'm suggesting is this: Since remaining a unified whole as the Church is vital to us as believers, we should be willing to practice taking this pause to evaluate our heart before acting on an interpretation, even though it is difficult. I'm not naïve, it'll definitely require the grace of God operating within us to even practice this. But the pain from a schism within the body of Christ would be more devastating.

The prevention of ecclesiastical schismatic pain was on the hearts of early church men and women martyrs when they chose to endure physical pain and death in their own bodies.

MENTAL NOTE #5: What is the difference between a "non-essential" and "heresy".

MENTAL NOTE #6: Think of a few recurring faults that disrupt the unity among Christians in America today.

MENTAL NOTE #7: Let's say that you disagree with what someone has said. What's your challenge to pausing to evaluate your own heart before responding based on your initial interpretation?

Chapter 3: Maintain Course Integrity

For the most part, each Christian factions use some of the same words, phrases, scriptures and talking points. But often, what is not spoken is the basis, motive and the hopes behind what we have spoken. It is crucial to consider that, as well as the speaker's faith community, in order to understand effectively. We should first ask ourselves, "Is the speaker using the same words, phrases, scriptures and talking points, to express the same principles and the same motives as the Bible?" Second, "Do their motives align with mine?" If not, "What should I do about the differences in motives?"

There are several religious factions in America claiming to be Christian, using the same words, phrases, scriptures and talking points, yet they are not spiritually grounded where you are, nor are they praying for the same outcomes as you. Do not judge them, just recognize them by their fruit (Matthew 7:15-23). Answers to the previous questions helps to identify with whom to remain unified, as a whole, to the Church - the body of Christ.

When doing so, we must remember the words of the 17th century German Lutheran theologian, Rupertus Meldenius (aka Peter Meiderlin or Peter Meuderlinus), during the Thirty Years War - "*In essentials unity, in non-essentials liberty, in all things charity.*"[1]

The Essentials

1. Unity of the Father, the Son, and the Holy Spirit in the Godhead.

2. Sovereignty of God in creation, revelation, redemption, and final judgment.

3. Divine inspiration of Scripture; its infallibility as originally given; its sole authority, complete sufficiency, in all matters of faith and conduct.

4. Universal sinfulness and guilt of human nature since the fall, rendering men and women subject to God's wrath and condemnation.

5. Redemption from the guilt, penalty, and power of sin only through the sacrificial death as our representative and substitute of Jesus Christ, the incarnate Son of God.

6. Literal physical resurrection of Jesus from the dead

7. Work of the Holy Spirit to make the death of Jesus effective to the individual sinner, granting him repentance towards God and faith in

8. Jesus Christ.

9. Indwelling work of the Holy Spirit in the believer.

10. One holy universal church, which is the body of Christ and to which all true believers belong (dead and living).

11. Expectation of the personal return of the Lord Jesus Christ in power and in glory.

MENTAL NOTE #8: How did ancient sea-faring navigators travel with great accuracy?

MENTAL NOTE #9: *What is your north star? Describe a situation that was difficult to follow it, but you did so anyway.*

Chapter 4: Trust the Instrumentation

Scriptures of the Bible are the errorless Word of God (as He led men to write). It should be read and followed as the Christian source of authority. Because Adam, as the federal head of humanity, disobeyed God, our world is fallen, corrupt and evil. But rather than fix the earth, God will destroy it and bring about a new heaven and earth. Until then, Jesus has commissioned His Church (believers) to spread the good news of salvation, in order to make disciples (Matthew 28:18-20). This is the Church's chief mission. Because to die without accepting Christ as personal savior, for the forgiveness of sin, will result in spending an eternity in torturous punishment (also known as hell).

Though Jesus has gone ahead of us to His Father to prepare a heavenly place for us, we have been left "in this world", but our values and hope are not of this world." We are to live as though Jesus will return to gather us (both dead in Christ and alive) with Him. Left behind will be those refused to accept His salvation for forgiveness of sin.

However, as previously stated, to understand what a Christian believes an understanding of the broader context of their faith community is required. Answers to the previously posed questions would help tremendously. Why? Because factions such as, Christian Nationalists, Christian Social/Political Activist and Carnal Christians all consent to the essentials of the faith. "Isn't that a good thing? ", you might ask. The answer could be "Yes" or "Maybe. " Considering Jesus' assessment in Matthew chapter, the motives in a person's heart, methods, objectives and spiritual walk might reveal a departure from the kingdom perspective.

> Jesus said in Matthew 7:21, *"Not everyone who says to me, 'Lord, Lord,' will enter the kingdom of heaven, but only the one who does the will of my Father who is in heaven."*

The nature of today's prominent Christian voices is nationalistic, social, political, activistic, and carnal. And then there is the Christ-centered message of the Bible. The confusion that these factions pose to an undiscerning ear is similar to the confusion in grammar with homophonic and homographic homonyms. They use similar and familiar words and phraseology when proclaiming the gospel and end-time message. Yet, each has different motives and hopes when doing so.

<u>Bible's Gospel and End-Time Message</u>

This is what the inspired Word of God has declared and promised.

Motive – To save people from the condition, penalty and punishment of sin (Matthew 1:21).

Advocates/Priorities
- Forgiveness is through Jesus' redemptive work on the cross.

- Individual's heartful belief and confession that Jesus is Lord and Savior (Romans 3:23-25; 9:10-11).

- In order to make disciples in all nations, teach them to obey Christ (Matthew 28:18-20).

Hope/Objectives

- God the Father be glorified

- Christ to increase the number of believers (Acts 2:42-47)

- Believers to be cleansed by God's truth (John 17:16-18)

- To rule with Christ and live eternally with Him (Jude 20-22; Revelation 20:4)

Sadly, each Christian faction has made the biblical message secondary to their agenda (or has elevated a non-essential to an essential). What they have not articulated is, an authoritative revelation that prompts them to do so?

MENTAL NOTE #10: When the biblical message aligns with your primary agenda, then you are navigating accurately. What are some temptations to veering off course?

Let's peek behind each faction's terminology, deeds, and what they have shared or displayed publicly. This helps us to gain a summary understanding of their motives, advocacy, priorities, hopes and objectives.

Christian Nationalists

In many circles lately, this label has been generally applied to a spectrum of predominately Caucasian Christians who desire to "make" America a Christian nation (based on beliefs said to be of America's founding fathers).[2] The ease with which this faction tends to treat the biblical message as secondary to their national ambitions is noteworthy. For the most part, its views have been forged through a history of American exploitation, conquest, the Doctrine of Discovery and privilege.[3]

This will be more evident as we dive deeper into their motives, methods, and objectives of Christian Nationalist.

Their Motive – To restore America to its past glorious days when authority was `exclusively controlled by Caucasian Christian men. The ideology informing their motives has more to do with historic identity, cultural primacy and political influence than advocacy for Christian beliefs and doctrine. Their advocacy is for "America First" policies.

What they Advocate or Prioritize
- In his book, "*Preparing for War: The Extremist History of White Christian Nationalism*", Bradley Onishi describes their views this way – "... prioritizes patriotism over compassion, national defense over

loving one's neighbor, and protecting the unborn more than loving anyone on earth." He goes on to describe his own experience with "trusting pastors and elders whose faith inspired me to forgo critical thought for radical obedience [by "stopping the steal"].

- Waging war against school curriculums.

- Maintaining traditional Caucasian-American family values.

- Declaring any group/individual that advocates for social or political rights/reform to be socialists.

- Under the guise of radical obedience to God, they riot, lie, obstruct, manipulate, and violate justice and order.

Their Hope or Objectives –
- To carry out what they believe to be a God given duty to prevent America from ruin due to, what they have identified as, the unbiblical agendas of Christian social/political activists, carnal Christians, and secular humanists.

- Civil war, if necessary.

- That America's governing laws and principles become Christian based, thereby allowing freedom to worship Christ and study the Bible, in public, private and government institutions.

MENTAL NOTE #11: What strongholds keep you entrenched in a nationalistic agenda?

MENTAL NOTE #12: What would it take to let go and trust Christ to address those strongholds?

Christian Social/Political Activists

This is a label use by Christian Nationalists when referring to the spectrum of Christians who do not share nationalist views. Instead, this faction seeks to "make" America more equitable and opportunistic for all ethnic, age, sex, economic and political classes. Despite the overwhelming number of Christians (both Caucasian and African American) in American history who have risked their lives for freedom and civil rights, this faction tends to treat the biblical message as secondary to social and political gains to be made within American systems. They are more humanistic, than they are nationalistic, or Christian. Their views have been forged by over 400 years as victims of exploitation, subjugation, slavery, oppressive legislation and second-class citizenship.

This will become more evident as we dive deeper into their motives, methods, and objectives

Their Motive
- Extend the same rights and equity enjoyed by Caucasian citizens (legal, education, housing, employment, politics, etc.) to racial minority and other excluded citizens.

- Sustain and expand rights to women that their male counterparts enjoy.

- Make structural changes to empower local communities.

- Ensure fair distribution of resources to communities.

What they Advocate or Prioritize
- Economic determinism over sanctity of life

regarding abortion

- Self-identity over Imago Dei regarding sex and gender

- Equality in reparations (slave owners received them, slaves never have)

- Reform in policing

Their Hope or Objectives
- An America in which all citizens and immigrants have equal opportunity and access to life, liberty and the pursuit of happiness.

- Prays that America's leaders to allow the freedom of self-affirmation and to worship as one pleases.

MENTAL NOTE #13: What strongholds keep you entrenched as an activist?

MENTAL NOTE #14: What would it take to let go and trust Christ to address those strongholds?

Carnal Christians

This label has been liberally applied to the spectrum of Christians who, though they profess the biblical message, show little or no remorse, nor repentance for biblical sins of omission or commission. This faction also includes Christians with an unbiblical level of emphasis on persona, profit or platform. They tend to have a limited understanding of Christian essentials, and instead treat the Bible simply as a set of suggestions. For them, the biblical message as secondary to their human experience, feelings, ambitions, and secular pursuits. Many individuals in this faction may very well have observed how the other two factions rendered the biblical message as secondary. Then, in like fashion, they too rendered the biblical message secondary to their personal pleasures and interests.

As in the case with the other two factions, let's dive deeper into the motives, methods and objectives of this group.

Their Motive – To place self or secular interests before the greatest commandment and the golden rule (Matthew 22:36-40; Luke 6:30-32), embrace materialism, and indulge in sinful human desires.

What they Advocate or Prioritize – Theirs are fluid and often change, depending on the pressing needs or popularity of the times. However, two attributes that seem to be constant among this faction are:
- Anti-intellectualism, which prefers entertainment over intellectual stimulation, to a fault.

- The tendency to measure the value of something (usually their time and comfort) based on how much personal or material gain can be had.

Their Hope or Objectives – To accumulate sufficiency for living, in order to enjoy the rewards during earthly life.

MENTAL NOTE #15: What strongholds keep you focused on comfort, pursuing wealth and/or accumulating material items?

MENTAL NOTE #16: What would it take to pursue God's agenda first, then trust Christ for the lifestyle that He has for you?

Twice in the biblical message all believers have been warned that, "There is a way that appears to be right, but in the end it leads to death." (Proverbs 14:12; 16:25).

Keeping Jesus Primary

No matter how noble the attempt to restore or to reform America, human pride on the part of either faction keeps the danger of national death lingering over America. As is often the case, before death, there is pain. Before pain, there is danger. The 21st century church in America is flirting with danger – danger from not abiding in Christ. Putting Him second to our agendas will render us useless. Which is why in John 15:5, Jesus said, "apart from me you can do nothing".

Pain results when we ignore the signs of danger. Jesus goes on to say in verse six, "If you do not remain in me, you are like a branch that is thrown away and withers; such branches are picked up, thrown into the fire and burned." Note that, being able to "do nothing" includes restoring or reforming America.

Biblical and church history is filled with factions of God's people who miserably broke off into one scandalous faction to the next. Some examples are:

- King Rehoboam vs. Jeroboam in 1 Kings 12:1-24)
- The handling of the lapsi, Donatists vs. Catholics
- The Synod of the Corpse, the East-West Schism
- The Thirty-Years War, etc.

The disappointing truth is that, allegations against one faction upon the others didn't need be true to cause pain within the entire body of Christ.

Chapter 5: Schism Cycle Awareness

More important than national ambitions, social reform, or personal satisfaction, is that the Church be a universal and unified whole – one in Christ; even at the risk of regional extinction. That's what is at risk when we relegate the biblical message as secondary to our agenda. By doing so, it becomes much easier for church members to feel anesthetized against the pain caused to the Church body. Hiding behind seemingly supportive bible verses while advocating our agenda, only creates a false sense of obedience to God.

The basic Bible study principle that scripture does not cancel out other scriptures is helpful here. When it seems like they do, God (not us) makes them clear elsewhere in scripture. Omnisciently, Jesus' kingdom agenda has already taken our concerns into consideration, then still made His word primary. He inspired men to write them down! So, let's just obey that! For us to make this nation Christian, or to make it equitable, at the expense of the biblical message, and then call ourselves the Church, is nonsense!

Sure, we have been commanded to make disciples - but not to force an increase in our numbers through agendas and gimmicks. Rather, by teaching theology in addition to preaching, abiding in Christ, and remaining a universal and unified whole that embraces the biblical message. Then, the Lord will cause the increase to a number of His choosing (Acts 2:42-47). Do not let the devil trick us into hurting the Church with a schism.

An honest assessment of the ecclesiological and Christological state of the church in America, should convict believers of nothing less than torturing the Lord's body. Nonetheless, human pride (be it national, in one's identity, or in self) has paralyzed us from prioritizing ecclesiological and Christological matters over personal or factional motives. In contrast to 1 Corinthians 13:13, this American pride has traded hope that is centered in Christ, for a hope in humanist agendas. It has devalued the greatest commandment to love God and neighbor above self. It has callously disrupted the bond of love towards others, and it has demoted faith to second chair.

For similar pain in the body of Christ, the early African Church father and scholar Augustine of Hippo despised the schism of the 4th and 5th centuries A.D. [4] The prideful state of today's church in American is strikingly similar to what led North African Donatist Christians and Rome's Nicaean Christians, in his era, to permit a painful ecclesiological and Christological schism to wreak havoc.

Looping to the 4th – 5th Centuries A.D.

From the 4th through 5th centuries A.D., the once universally whole Christian Church battled within. After the Edict of Milan in 313 A.D., many congregations within the Roman Empire (primarily in northwest Africa and some in Spain and Italy) dissented against the Roman Empire's newly formed church-state union. Their congregations were not included on Emperor Constantine's Benevolence List (for reparations due to persecution). Religious/political protests of one dissenting group, labelled Donatists, grew within the church like a ravaging cancer.

Donatists experienced a devastating blow in 380 A.D., when the Roman emperors Theodosius I, Gratian, and Valentinian II issued the Edict of Thessalonica (without consulting the church). The edict declared Nicaean Christianity the state religion of the Roman Empire. The emperors then reserved the term *Catholic* to mean Nicaean Christianity. Though forty-five years prior, Donatists believed their interests had not been represented at the Nicaean council, there were no doctrinal nor ecclesiological differences between them and Nicaeans. This is evidenced by the fact that during the First Nicaean Council in 325 A.D. Donatist teachings were not deemed to be heresy and none of their clergy were found to be heretics.

Still, the Edict of Thessalonica alienated Donatist Christians from empire-wide Christian life. Donatists did, however, differ in practices and application, particularly when it came to graveyard ceremonies and recognizing the qualifications of clergy (non-essentials). For some time, especially during Augustine's lifetime, Donatists were in the majority, but Catholics had the power of the Roman Empire on their side.

- Was the Donatists' popularity a political threat to Nicaeans?

- Were the Donatists' different practices and application that big of a threat to the newly formed, empire wide, church-state union?

- Was the new definition for *Catholic* a power play by the emperors to neutralize the influence of Northwest Africa Christian congregations?

I do not have the answers to those questions. What is clear is that the ecclesiological and Christological wear from protests, in-fighting, and suffering within the body of Christ made it susceptible to outside attacks.

MENTAL NOTE #17: Think about outside threats to the American way of life (climate, terrorism, political, declining dollar, challenges to democracy, disease). Does Christian in-fighting mitigate or exacerbate them?

MENTAL NOTE #18: Do you know why other factions do not support your faction's views?

MENTAL NOTE #19: Why do you believe the other factions are wrong?

Deception of Might As Right

Shortly after the Edict of Thessalonica, there was a military coup within the empire. Gildo the son of the Moorish Berber King Nubel, an African, was promoted to both Roman General and Magistrate of Africa's northwestern region, where he served the interests of Emperor Theodosius I. After the emperor's death, in 395 A.D., General Gildo seized the opportunity to take control of African territories colonized by Rome. He declared their independence and attempted to restore North Africa to its former glory.[5] This heightened Catholic fears. They accelerated repressive legislation against the Donatists by keeping pressure on the imperial courts for more anti-Donatist legislation, as well as financial and civic penalties.

Several decades later, in 429 A.D., the Vandals invaded northwest Africa; with help from the Moors. Rome abdicated its territories in northwest Africa, and both Donatist and Catholic Christians were persecuted for their Trinitarian beliefs. Without the support of the Roman Empire, Nicaean congregations in northwest Africa unsuccessfully defended themselves. Donatists, however, took refuge among their native African Berber countrymen. The Vandals occupied northwest Africa for the next 100 years.

In her book, *Vanished Cities of Northern Africa*, Steuart Erskine describes the devastation to the Early African Church, by the invading Vandal people, as follows:

"The Africa of their invasion was the Africa of Augustine [Bishop of Hippo] and many saintly people."

"Their [Vandals] rapacity knew no bounds, their

41

cruelty was abnormal and they laid waste and never rebuilt."

"They found Africa flourishing and left it desolate …"

"… its people reduced to slavery"

"The Church of Africa – so important in those early days of Christianity – practically non-existent."

In his book, *Christians and Muslims*, Dr. Noel Quinton King, founder of the University of California at Santa Cruz's Department of the History of Religion states:

"The main reason for the disappearance of Christianity in the northwest of the African continent may well have been the beauty of in-coming young Islam, compared with the tired Christianity left by the great struggle between Catholics and the others, eking out an existence in a society ruined by barbarian invasion and East Roman reconquest."

Chapter 6: No Real Winners

Sadly, the self-inflicted ecclesiological and Christological pain within the Christian Church, plunged Christianity into what has been labeled by historians as the Dark Ages (5th – 15th centuries A.D.). The profound lesson to take away from Church history is this: Making Nicaean Christianity the state religion of the empire did not create a formidable superpower from the union of the Christian God and the Roman Empire. Nor did Donatist social/political activism for meaningful representation and fair distribution of resources, bring about a change within the empire.

Shortly after the 380 A.D. Edict of Thessalonica, and continuing into the 5th century A.D., the national, social, political and religious bottoms fell for the Christian Church in the West.

- 13 years after the edict, Catholics pressured the Roman Empire for repressive legislature against Donatists.

- 15 years after the edict, Roman General Gildo successfully pulled off a coup of North African territories.

- 21 years after the edict, never again did Rome appoint a Berber or Donatist sympathizer to represent North Africa.

- 31 years after the edict, Rome passed more repressive legislature against the Donatists.

- 39 years after the edict, at the African Council in Carthage, Archbishop Augustine of Hippo, lost confidence in appealing to clergy in Rome.[6]

- 49 years after the edict, the Vandal invasion into northwest Africa began.

Vandals would rule there for 100 years.

- Catholics of Africa were abandoned by Rome, and then persecuted by the Vandals.

- Donatists in Africa were scattered, and then persecuted by the Vandals.

- The Dark Ages began.

- The church grew too weak to enforce its condemnation of Pelagianism in western Europe.

- The fall of the Roman Empire began.

- The self-inflicted ecclesiological and Christological pain contributed significantly to the disappearance of Christianity in northwest Africa.

- African scholarship and ecclesiastical leadership were lost.

Rome's declaration of being a Nicaean Christian Empire was short lived (not even 50 years). Though the Donatists were in the majority (and resisted Rome), their hope for justice was dashed. There were no winners. Regardless of sincere and noble efforts, God did not pick a side. Only disaster for both factions followed.

Are we repeating this unhealthy pattern in Western Christianity today? The tactical measures of Donatists and Nicaeans should have never taken precedence over Jesus' worldwide mission for the Church – be a universal and unified body that loves God and neighbor as self, and makes disciples (who themselves also makes disciples).

God Did Not Pick a Side

Remember in Joshua 5:13-15, as Joshua

approached the city of Jericho to overtake it? He saw a man in front of him with a drawn sword. Joshua asked, "Are you for us or for our enemies?"

"Neither," he replied, "but as commander of the army of the Lord I have now come."

The man turned out to be an angel assigned to carry out God's will, but not to take sides. So, it became imperative that Joshua do a self-examination, "Who's agenda am I advancing?"

The problem before 4th and 5th century Christians was never who was right. Was it the Christian nationalist Roman emperors or the social/political activist Donatists? Or, was the problem a lack of resolve by either faction to put being a universal unified body of Christ first and foremost – one that trusted that Jesus could work out the low-level details?

MENTAL NOTE #20: Church history shows that God does not take sides. How should this inform the tenacity in which you pursue your agenda?

**MENTAL NOTE #21: What prayer needs do you
have to help realign your agenda with the
biblical message?**

Chapter 7: Escaping the Schism Cycle

To avoid the same fate as the Donatists and Catholics, we who are the body of Christ should take time to sense Jesus' pain. Otherwise, while we are vulnerable, some outside entity could seize the occasion to cause our demise. Think about it, if either Christian faction today were to prevail, since neither has made the biblical message primary, then what would it matter? How would the God of the Bible support that faction?

The only real option is to swallow human pride, embrace being a universal, unified, body under the biblical message, then trust Jesus Christ to work out the rest. Without a doubt, it will be a tough pill to swallow. It is not that, what God expects of us is difficult. Rather, that since we have wandered so far from the primacy of the biblical message, and for so long, we've made it difficult on our egos to be as God expects. It is our own attachment to sinful pride that makes it tough to get back to where God wants us.

The Case for Deference

I used to think that church history was progressive - like an upward trending sloped line depicting ecclesiastical improvements with the passage of time. Unfortunately, both biblical and post-biblical church history shows it to be circular. Today, it seems that the church has come upon its old footprints. I believe embracing the principle of deference would help provide a course of correction.

Deference towards the kingdom of God can help the church avoid repeating past mistakes. Because, when it comes to remediating painful matters with each other as brothers and sisters in Christ, it is not enough to be correct. It is far more beneficial, when necessary, to defer to the greater good of God's kingdom. The principle of deferring to a greater kingdom good is the motive behind what Jesus and His apostles taught, regarding handling conflicts and differences.

Here are a few ways their teachings challenge us as believers.

- Turning the other cheek

- Suffering loss rather than taking a brother or sister to court

- The strong bearing the infirmities of the weak

- Not returning evil for evil

- Not avenging ourselves. Like the restraint David showed against King Saul; and as the Apostles taught

- Obeying Pharisees because they sat in Moses' seat

- If someone takes your coat, give them your shirt also

Often, against the very fiber of their being, mature kingdom believers will defer acting on a response that would provide some personal satisfaction, if doing so reflects badly on the kingdom of God. For believers, being perceived as the unified whole body of Christ is far more beneficial to the kingdom, than it is for us - as an individual - to be perceived as being correct, vindicated or on the right side. Unfortunately, human pride and arrogance too often preclude us from deferring to the greater good of the kingdom. This is a reason why God hates pride (Proverbs 8:13). Deference is the missing variable in today's formula for unity in the body of Christ.

Beneficiaries of Deference in Others

Let me first say that deference is not tolerating sin amongst brothers and sisters in Christ. Doing that would reflect badly on the kingdom of God. Biblical church discipline clearly calls for sin to be addressed. Through discipline, we are deferring to the Lord's ability to restore the person. This is particularly true when a believer refuses to acknowledge that their act, behavior, or thought is sinful, even after being shown that the Bible clearly shows that it is.

Be careful, though. Because, *how* we show deference is as essential as actually showing it. Handling a brother or sister who has fallen to sin is a delicate manner. Feelings are on sleeves, skin is thin, and pins and needle are under bare feet! So, begin with the realization that their repentance (and not our rebuke) is key to his/her maintaining a healthy fellowship with Christ. Consider the following scenarios:

Scenario #1 - I sin and acknowledge that it is an offense against Christ. Conviction sets in, and then I repent in my heart and turn around. That's it, as far as my fellowship with Christ is concerned (except, if I am a church leader there may be more involved). Rather than berate me, I would want others to show deference to what Scripture says about my repentance and the fruit thereof.

Scenario #2 - When I struggle with

overcoming a sin, even after repenting, and get structured help through counseling and have praying accountability partners, I would want others to show deference toward my structured process. Allow me to experience deliverance, not humiliation.

Scenario #3 - As a new Christian struggling with walking out my newness in Christ, I will waver between my old-self and my new-self. I would want others to show deference to what Scripture says about how, with love the mature men and women come along side to teach younger men and women. Teach me from the Word of God and the testimony of how you overcame the old nature. Trust that I will mature spiritually.

Scenario #4 – You and I may be at opposite poles on the "scale of passion" about current events. We are stubborn and will not budge. It could be a matter of maturity, credibility, access to information, or a difference in point of reference about things. We need to show deference to the notion of unity in the essentials, liberty in nonessentials, and in all things, love.

However, in order to show deference in those scenarios, our souls will need a good spiritual cleansing. Because in our current condition, we are either attempting to save America by aggressively restoring her to a prior state of brokenness, or trying to reform her to be a just nation apart from the Lord, upon whom justice is based. We must first repent, then show one another more grace. Being created in God's image, let's go about saving and restoring America, with respect for that image.

Others Benefit from Our Deference

Ask yourself, Do I pass Jesus' eye test? Because He wants to replace the darkness within the human soul with His light. He has declared,

> "The eye is the lamp of the body. If your eyes are healthy, your whole body will be full of light. But if your eyes are unhealthy, your whole body will be full of darkness. If then the light within you is darkness, how great is that darkness!" Matthew 6:22-23

Our mind's eye is our perception. Healthy means, it illuminates godly understanding. But when dimly lit, it is unhealthy. A dimly lit perception renders us susceptible to darkness – which would prevent us from understanding events or people in healthy ways. Even worst, the darkness from a dimly lit perception inhibits our willingness, and subsequently our ability, to show deference to what the Word of God teaches. So, when the mind has been informed by the Word of God, not only do we mature spiritually, but we will have the proper basis for sorting through what's essential and non-essential to the Christian faith. Thereby, as a diverse body of brothers and sisters in Christ, we could still act as a unified whole.

On the surface this may sound naïve. But then, much of what the Bible asks of us sounds naïve, that is, until the Lord's supernatural provisions are considered on a personal level. It is at this level where we discover that our obedience is better than anything we can sacrifice to Him (1 Samuel 15:22).

Our present perception of the minutest of things is molded by our past experiences. This includes the meaning we ascribe to what we have experienced and seen, and to a lesser degree to the experiences of others. Applying the 1988 "Windows and Mirrors" framework developed by the educator Emily Styles,[7] helps explain how our experiences on a personal level function as *windows and mirrors of life*. Having gazed into them, what we take away will greatly determine how we interpret similar events in the future. This is especially true when it involves people with different viewpoints than us.

Whatever illuminates our perception (which can vary in degree of clarity) will influence our future significantly. Dark words and deeds resulting from a dimly lit perception can destroy our willingness to show deference. While, the courage that results from a godly illuminated perception will promote obedience. The Bible is full of examples of what dimly lit perceptions. I'll categorize them under windows and mirrors.

MENTAL NOTE #22: How would you want to be treated after discovering that your agenda was not tightly aligned with God's plan?

MENTAL NOTE #23: Could you treat others the same way, when they discovered their agenda was not tightly aligned with God's plan?

DIMLY LIT WINDOW OBSERVATIONS

Windows are those occasions when, as a passerby, we see the deeds of others. Our mishandling of these windows can result in inaccurate perceptions. For a mental picture, consider how the author equates his love to a naïve doe that gazes into windows in the Song of Solomon 2:9.

> "My beloved is like a gazelle or a young stag. Look! There he stands behind our wall, gazing through the windows, peering through the lattice."

Here are three ways we misinterpret the deeds of others when simply gazing:

- We formulate an opinion or narrative based on the snippet of what we see, without consideration for the events that led up to or follow what we have peeped.

- We use values and beliefs from our personal, family or cultural experiences, to assess virtue or corruption in the words or deeds of others; as though our experiences are a standard for gauging others.

- We feel compelled to take a side. Even though we do not understand what we see (or what it means), and then make rash judgments.

But also, there are windows where we look intently at others with an ill-intent (as in Daniel 6:10-12).

> "Now when Daniel learned that the decree had been published, he went home to his upstairs

room where the windows opened toward Jerusalem. Three times a day he got down on his knees and prayed, giving thanks to his God, just as he had done before. Then these men went as a group and found Daniel praying and asking God for help. So they went to the king and spoke to him about his royal decree: "Did you not publish a decree that during the next thirty days anyone who prays to any god or human being except to you, Your Majesty, would be thrown into the lions' den?"

Here, while gazing, we filter what we see through a preconceived idea of the kind of person they are, and their possible motive. We hone in on words or deeds that confirm our preconception, and become deaf and blinded to words and deeds that do not confirm our preconception.

DIMLY LIT MIRROR OBSERVATIONS

Mirrors are those occasions where we have considered ourself in the situation that we are gazing into. In the moment, we either - with an illuminated perception - allowed empathy to temper our interpretation about the person in our view, or - with a dimly lit perception - we fall somewhere between apathy and contempt for the person in our view.

Here too, are ways that our mishandling of mirrors can result in inaccurate perceptions. For a mental picture, consider James 1:22-24, also Proverbs 27:19).

"Do not merely listen to the word, and so deceive yourselves. Do what it says. Anyone who listens to the word but does not do what it says is like someone who looks at his face in a mirror and, after looking at himself, goes away and immediately forgets what he looks like."

Here are five ways we selectively put-up blinders that can stunt our spiritual growth (the forgetfulness that James mentions).

- Failure to turn over our own personal shame issues to Jesus for forgiveness can prevent us from perceiving the person we are viewing as being forgivable.

- Failure to consider that our Father is also the Father of people who are different than us.

- Contempt in our heart prevents us from treating others as we would want to be treated, had we been in the same situation.

- Taking a stand for justice and equity, while being unjust ourselves towards God in the use of the time, service, skills, money, influence and possessions that He has allowed us to have (be it in our poverty or abundance).

- We want God's blessing to make our nation great, yet we cover our ears and turn away as our nation's lack of support to help developing nations grow industrially and gain economic independence.

Also, mirrors are those occasions when we go on the offense against things that we too have been guilty of, but somehow have justified ourselves. Three examples of this are:
- When we advocate or pray for the eradication of evil doers, when we have yet to be saved loved ones. How can God

eradicate evil without eradicating our unsaved love ones?

- We seek to "cancel" people for hypocrisy. Yet, we are well aware of the hypocrisy in us when no one is looking. God is always looking!

- We protest against the mistreatment and exploitation of the poor, work-a-day citizens and animals, while at the same time we disdain morality and exploit the body of Christ, through willful and intentional sins.

In summary, we cannot get along with people, effectively, who are different than us without first overcoming the darkness within us – *which is, an unwillingness to fully surrender to the biblical worldview.* This was especially true for me! Many of our presumptions and thoughts will need to be taken captive and made obedient to Christ (2 Corinthians 10:5). It is not something we will like to do. It will certainly take courage.

Deference Yields Space to the Divine

With deference in the previous scenarios, we mustn't anguish over our sin. It is the Holy Spirit's task to address the sin, through sanctification. All parties involved must not only turn it over to the Lord in prayer, but each must be willing to accept what the Lord does with our situation. Most often, the outcome is quite different from what either party would have imagined.

That was my experience. I came out of retirement to take a job helping an international Christian organization make information security process improvements. Though the organization, and individuals there, had different views than me on many national newsworthy matters, we were in complete agreement about the essentials of the Christian faith. We would break from work for department prayer and homily sessions weekly. On several occasions, I led those sessions myself. Throughout my stay there, I never felt pressured to embrace a viewpoint on current events that was different from mine, nor a viewpoint that was contrary to the essential of the faith.

Staff members were diverse and friendly. We worked around my quirks, and their idiosyncrasies, while meshing our personalities. Now having said that, I am certain there were many occasions where deference was employed, by each of us. It never rose to a level where someone felt diminished or devalued as a person. But having set it aside to allow the Lord to deal with it, we pressed forward.

When the Lord solved the matter, I quietly rejoiced. But most often, speaking for myself, the passage of time changed my perspective. It afforded me an opportunity to get to know the people involved better (personally and professionally). Also, it allowed me to understand that what I believed to be problematic, was just a different way to arrive at the same end. Misunderstanding was often due to constraints (both organizational and personal) of which I was unaware. Overall, we worked well together. We still keep in touch!

Remain in Christ

Let's say that Jesus returned today to begin His eschatological agenda (about which, we only know in part, 1 Corinthians 13:12). Consider the following list of virtues. Which do you think would have prepared you for an eternity with Him? Rank them according to how they align with His agenda. Realize, that one virtue may exist to the benefit of another. But which would be a means and which an end? Here are the virtues:

- Deferring to His teachings (reverence for Christ)

- Getting along with your neighbor (love involves extending grace to others)

- Showing humility (subduing pride)

- Devotion to Christian nationalism

- Devotion to social/political justice

- Self-fulfillment

In closing, I am not suggesting that by deferring to the will of God, in our dealings with other, today's problems will go away. Though some problems may. What I do believe is, doing so would create a more palatable mind-heart dynamic among diverse Christian factions. A dynamic that affords us a better vantage from which to view our problems, as well as position us for the divine illumination that is necessary to understand how solutions should look. We can do our part, as the Lord's instruments, to help the 21st century church avoid a repeat of the schisms in its past.

Finally, let's not minimize the truth that the kingdom of God has confidence in the word of God. The power of His word functions reflectively as a mirror, as well as introspectively as a window into the soul. So, also remember this:

When the believer hears or reads the word of God, and then responds trusting what it says, the word will help him or her to trust it more.

But when the believer hears or reads the word of God, and then reacts to it with indifference, apathy or self-pride, the word will harden his or her heart in their indifference, apathy or self-pride.

Through various windows of life, as the world gaze at believers, our deferring to the word of God, when dealings with one another, will let them know that we are Jesus' disciples.

MENTAL NOTE #24: When in a disagreement with someone, what virtue(s) might help you to leave room for God, out of deference?

MENTAL NOTE #25: In what instances or subjects do you need more grace to leave room for God?

About the Author

Pastor Jimmie D. Compton, Jr and his wife Nancy have two children, two grandchildren, and two great-grandchildren. Received his Masters of Arts degree in Pastoral Counseling at Ashland Theological Seminary, and was licensed as a therapist. He founded and served as Senior Pastor of Hope Bible Fellowship Church for thirty years. Pastor Compton also provided counseling services while with the Detroit Police Chaplain Corps, Detroit Rescue Mission Ministries and Eastwood Clinic. He has aided other church leaders with counseling and ministerial needs, while authoring several books.

Pastor Compton has been honored for completing in-depth, six-year research into Early African Church History: From Jesus' Birth to the Rise of Islam. This research has been embraced by church leaders and developed into a two-year, online, self-paced curriculum by Hope Institute, the teaching and ministerial arm of Hope Bible Fellowship Church.

For more information, or for bulk copies of this book at a discount, email us with "About IATL" in the subject at hbf.church@gmail.com.

Honorable Mentions

inkBlaze Media's review of *In All Things, Love: Escaping the Church Schism Cycle* states, "addresses pressing issues within the modern Christian Church, reflecting on historical parallels while offering a transformative perspective rooted in Jesus' kingdom message. Your book's deep exploration of these topics resonates profoundly in today's cultural and religious climate.

Your ability to blend historical analysis with actionable wisdom and personal narrative creates a compelling and relatable reading experience. The board was especially impressed by how you shed light on complex theological and cultural dynamics with clarity and passion.

With a background as a pastor, counselor, and community leader, your insights are not only well-informed but also grounded in decades of practical ministry and leadership. Your unique journey—from Detroit's eastside to a respected voice of faith—brings authenticity and authority to your work.

Endnotes

The citations and bibliography regarding accounts in this book about the issues that caused the dissent of Donatist congregations, as well as their ensuing clashes with Nicaeans, Catholics, Vandals and Byzantinians, can be found in my book, *Surveying Christianity's African Roots*, on Amazon.

---

[1] Schaff, Phillip, 'History of the Christian Church' Vol. 7, Grand Rapids: W.M. Eerdmans, 1910, pp650-653

[2] Onishi, Bradley, 'Preparing For War' Minneapolis: Broadleaf Books, 2023, Kindle ebook

[3] Provoledo, Elisabetta (31 March 2023). "Vatican Repudiates 'Doctrine of Discovery,' Used as Justification for Colonization". *New York Times.* Retrieved 1 April 2023.

[4] Monroe, Ty, 'Putting on Christ' Washington D.C.: The Catholic University of America Press, 2022, pp238-239

[5] Tilley, Maureen, 'The Bible in Christian North Africa', Minneapolis: Fortress Press, 1997, p132

[6] Peterson, John Bertram. "Apiarius of Sicca." The Catholic Encyclopedia. Vol. 1. New York: Robert Appleton Company, 1907. <http://www.newadvent.org/cathen/01594a.htm>.

[7] Style, Emily, 'Listening for All Voices', Summit: Oak Knoll School monograph, 1988

www.ingramcontent.com/pod-product-compliance
Lightning Source LLC
Chambersburg PA
CBHW060536030426
42337CB00021B/4292